CROCK·POT.

◆ THE ORIGINAL SLOW COOKER ◆

SOUPS & STEWS

Publications International, Ltd.

pilcookbooks.com

Louis Weber, CEO
Publications International, Ltd.
7373 North Cicero Avenue
Lincolnwood, IL 60712

Pictured on the front cover: Mexican Cheese Soup *(page 98)*.
Pictured on the back cover (clockwise from top): Linguiça & Green Bean Soup *(page 76)*, Cauliflower Soup *(page 8)* and Asian Beef Stew *(page 88)*.

ISBN-13: 978-1-4127-2940-6
ISBN-10: 1-4127-2940-8

Library of Congress Control Number: 2008924183

Manufactured in China.

8 7 6 5 4 3 2 1

pilcookbooks.com

TABLE OF CONTENTS

INTRODUCTION

Slow Cooking Hints and Tips

Slow Cooker Sizes

Smaller slow cookers, such as 1- to 3½-quart models, are the perfect size for singles, a couple, empty-nesters and for serving dips.

While medium-size slow cookers (those holding somewhere between 3 and 5 quarts) will easily cook enough food to feed a small family, they're also convenient for holiday side dishes and appetizers.

Large slow cookers are great for big family dinners, holiday entertaining, and potluck suppers. A 6- to 7-quart model is ideal if you like to make meals in advance and have dinner tonight and store leftovers for another day.

Types of Slow Cookers

Current models of **CROCK-POT®** slow cookers come equipped with many different features and benefits, from auto-cook programs, to stovetop-safe stoneware, to timed programming. Visit www.crockpot. com to find the slow cooker that best suits your needs and lifestyle.

Cooking, Stirring, and Food Safety

CROCK-POT® slow cookers are safe to leave unattended. The outer heating base may get hot as it cooks, but it should not pose a fire hazard. The heating element in the heating base functions at a low wattage and

is safe for your countertops.

Your slow cooker should be filled at least one-half to three-quarters full for most recipes unless otherwise instructed. Lean meats, such as chicken or pork tenderloin, will cook faster than meats with more connective tissue and fat, such as beef chuck or pork shoulder. Bone-in meats will take longer than boneless cuts. Typical slow cooker dishes take 7 to 8 hours to reach the simmer point on LOW and 3 to 4 hours on HIGH. Once the vegetables and meat begin to simmer and braise, their flavors will fully blend and the meat will become fall-off-the bone tender.

According to the United States Department of Agriculture, all bacteria are killed at a temperature of 165°F. It's important to follow the recommended cooking times and to avoid opening the lid often, especially early in the cooking process when heat is building up inside the unit. If you need to open the lid to check on your food or are adding additional ingredients, remember to allow additional cooking time, if necessary, to ensure food is thoroughly cooked and tender.

Large slow cookers, the 6- to 7-quart sizes, may benefit from a quick stir halfway through the cook time to help distribute heat and promote even cooking. It is usually unnecessary to stir at all since even ½ cup of liquid will help to distribute heat, and the crockery is the perfect medium for holding food at an even temperature throughout the cooking process.

Oven-Safe

All **CROCK-POT®** slow cooker removable crockery inserts may (without their lids) be used in

ovens at up to 400°F safely. Also, all **CROCK-POT®** crockery inserts are microwavable without their lids. If you own another brand slow cooker, please refer to your owner's manual for advice on oven and microwave safety.

Frozen Food

Frozen or partially frozen food can be cooked in a slow cooker; however, it will require a longer cooking time than the same recipe made with fresh food. Using an instant-read thermometer is recommended to ensure meat is completely cooked.

Pasta and Rice

If you're converting a recipe that calls for uncooked pasta, cook the pasta according to the package directions just until tender before adding it to the slow cooker. If you are converting a recipe that calls for cooked rice, stir in the raw rice with other ingredients; add ¼ cup of extra liquid per ¼ cup of raw rice.

Beans

Beans must be softened completely before they're combined with sugar and/or acidic foods. Sugar and acid have a hardening effect on beans and will prevent softening. Fully cooked canned beans may be used as a substitute for dried beans.

Vegetables

Root vegetables often cook more slowly than meat. Cut vegetables into small pieces so that they cook at the same rate as the meat, large or small, lean or marbled. Place them near the sides or on the bottom of the stoneware so that they will cook more quickly.

Herbs

Fresh herbs add flavor and color when they're added at the end of the cooking time, but for dishes with shorter cook times, hearty

fresh herbs such as rosemary and thyme hold up well. If added at the beginning, the flavor of many fresh herbs lessen over long cook times. Ground and/or dried herbs and spices work well in slow cooking because they retain their flavor, and may be added at beginning.

The flavor power of all herbs and spices can vary greatly depending on their particular strength and shelf life. Use chili powders and garlic powder sparingly because they often intensify over long cook times. Always taste the finished dish and adjust the seasonings, including salt and pepper, before serving.

Liquids

It's not necessary to use more than ½ to 1 cup of liquid in most instances since the juices in meats and vegetables are retained in slow cooking more so than in conventional cooking. Excess liquid can be reduced and concentrated after slow cooking either on the stovetop or by removing meat and vegetables from stoneware, stirring in cornstarch or tapioca, and setting the slow cooker to HIGH. Cook on

HIGH for approximately 15 minutes or until the juices are thickened.

Milk

Milk, cream, and sour cream break down during extended cooking. When possible, add them during the last 15 to 30 minutes of cooking, until just heated through. Condensed soups may be substituted for milk and can cook for extended times.

Fish

Fish is delicate and it should be stirred in gently during the last 15 to 30 minutes of cooking time. Cook just until cooked through, and serve immediately.

FAMILY FAVORITES

Cauliflower Soup

- **2** **heads cauliflower, cut into small florets**
- **8** **cups chicken broth**
- **¾** **cup chopped celery**
- **¾** **cup chopped onion**
- **2** **teaspoons salt**
- **2** **teaspoons black pepper**
- **2** **cups milk** *or* **light cream**
- **1** **teaspoon Worcestershire sauce**

1. Combine cauliflower, broth, celery, onion, salt and pepper in **CROCK-POT®** slow cooker. Cover; cook on LOW 7 to 8 hours or on HIGH 3 to 4 hours.

2. Using a hand mixer or hand blender, purée soup until smooth. Mix in milk and Worcestershire sauce, continuing to blend until smooth. Cook on HIGH 15 to 20 minutes longer before serving.

Makes 8 servings

Penne Pasta Zuppa

1 **can (15 ounces) white beans, drained and rinsed**

2 **medium yellow squash, diced**

2 **ripe tomatoes, diced**

2 **small red potatoes, cubed**

2 **leeks, sliced into quarters lengthwise then chopped**

1 **carrot, peeled and diced**

¼ **pound fresh green beans, washed, stemmed and diced**

2 **fresh sage leaves, minced**

1 **teaspoon salt**

½ **teaspoon black pepper**

8 **cups water**

¼ **pound uncooked penne pasta**

Grated Romano cheese (optional)

1. Combine beans, squash, tomatoes, potatoes, leeks, carrot, green beans, sage, salt and pepper in **CROCK-POT®** slow cooker. Add water. Stir well to combine. Cover; cook on HIGH 2 hours, stirring occasionally. Turn **CROCK-POT®** slow cooker to LOW. Cook, covered, 8 hours longer. Stir occasionally.

2. Turn **CROCK-POT®** slow cooker to HIGH. Add pasta. Cover; cook 30 minutes longer or until pasta is done.

3. To serve, garnish with Romano cheese, if desired.

Makes 6 servings

FAMILY FAVORITES

Manhattan Clam Chowder

3 slices bacon, diced

2 stalks celery, chopped

3 onions, chopped

2 cups water

1 can (15 ounces) stewed tomatoes, undrained and chopped

4 small red potatoes, diced

2 carrots, diced

½ teaspoon dried thyme

½ teaspoon black pepper

½ teaspoon Louisiana-style hot sauce

1 pound minced clams*

*If fresh clams are unavailable, use canned clams; 6 (6½-ounce) cans yield about 1 pound of clam meat; drain and discard liquid.

1. Cook and stir bacon in medium saucepan until crisp. Remove bacon and place in **CROCK-POT®** slow cooker.

2. Add celery and onions to skillet. Cook and stir until tender. Place in **CROCK-POT®** slow cooker.

3. Mix in water, tomatoes with juice, potatoes, carrots, thyme, pepper and hot sauce. Cover; cook on LOW 6 to 8 hours or HIGH 4 to 6 hours. Add clams during last half hour of cooking.

Makes 4 servings

Tip: *Shellfish and bivalves are delicate and should be added to the **CROCK-POT®** slow cooker during the last 15 to 30 minutes of the cooking time if you're using the HIGH heat setting, and during the last 30 to 45 minutes if you're using the LOW setting. This type of seafood overcooks easily, becoming tough and rubbery, so watch your cooking times, and cook only long enough for foods to be done.*

Curried Sweet Potato and Carrot Soup

2 medium-to-large sweet potatoes, peeled and cut into ¾-inch dice (about 5 cups)

2 cups baby carrots

1 small onion, chopped

¾ teaspoon curry powder

½ teaspoon salt, or to taste

½ teaspoon black pepper, or to taste

½ teaspoon ground cinnamon

¼ teaspoon ground ginger

4 cups chicken broth

1 tablespoon maple syrup

¾ cup half-and-half

Candied ginger (optional)

1. Place sweet potatoes, carrots, onion, curry powder, salt, pepper, cinnamon and ginger in **CROCK-POT®** slow cooker. Add chicken broth. Stir well to combine. Cover; cook on LOW 7 to 8 hours.

2. Pureé soup, 1 cup at a time, in blender, returning soup to **CROCK-POT®** slow cooker after each batch. (Or, use immersion blender.) Add maple syrup and half-and-half. Add salt and pepper, if desired. Cover; cook on HIGH 15 minutes to reheat. Serve in bowls and garnish with strips or pieces of candied ginger.

Makes 8 servings

Note: *Add 1 teaspoon of chicken soup base along with the broth for richer flavor.*

Potato Cheddar Soup

2 pounds red-skin potatoes, peeled and cut into ½-inch cubes

¾ cup coarsely chopped carrots

1 medium onion, coarsely chopped

3 cups chicken broth

½ teaspoon salt

1 cup half-and-half

¼ teaspoon black pepper

2 cups (8 ounces) shredded Cheddar cheese

1. Place potatoes, carrots, onion, broth and salt in **CROCK-POT®** slow cooker. Cover; cook on LOW 6 to 7 hours or on HIGH 3 to 3½ hours or until vegetables are tender.

2. Stir in half-and-half and pepper. Cover; cook on HIGH 15 minutes. Turn off heat and remove cover; let stand 5 minutes. Stir in cheese until melted.

Makes 6 servings

Serving suggestion: *Try this soup topped with whole wheat croutons.*

Granny's Apple Cidered Onion Soup with Gouda Cinnamon Toast

2 tablespoons olive oil

4 tablespoons butter, cubed, divided

4 medium to large onions, peeled and thinly sliced

2 medium Granny Smith apples, peeled, cored and chopped

4 cups chicken broth

1½ cups apple cider

2 tablespoons brandy (optional)

Salt and freshly ground black pepper, to taste

6 slices French *or* Italian bread, cut about ½ inch thick

2 tablespoons sugar

½ teaspoon ground cinnamon

2 cups shredded Gouda cheese, preferably aged

1. Spoon oil over bottom of **CROCK-POT®** slow cooker; add 2 tablespoons butter, distributing evenly. Add onions and apples. Cover; cook on LOW 8 to 10 hours or until onions are softened and caramelized.

2. Add broth, cider and brandy, if desired. Season with salt and black pepper. Cover; cook on HIGH about 1 hour or until hot.

3. While soup is heating, make Gouda Cinnamon Toast: Preheat broiler. Spread remaining 2 tablespoons softened butter on one side of bread slices. Combine sugar and cinnamon. Sprinkle evenly over buttered bread. Place bread on baking sheet and toast under broiler until golden brown.

4. Remove from oven; turn bread over and sprinkle untoasted side with Gouda cheese. Return to broiler until cheese melts, taking care not to burn.

5. To serve, ladle soup into bowls and float 1 piece Gouda Cinnamon Toast on top of each serving, cheese side up. Serve immediately.

Makes 6 servings

Butternut Squash-Apple Soup

3 packages (12 ounces each) frozen cooked winter squash, thawed and drained *or* about 4½ cups mashed cooked butternut squash

2 cans (about 14 ounces each) chicken broth

1 medium Golden Delicious apple, peeled, cored and chopped

2 tablespoons minced onion

1 tablespoon packed brown sugar

1 teaspoon minced fresh sage *or* ½ teaspoon ground sage

¼ teaspoon ground ginger

½ cup whipping cream *or* half-and-half

1. Combine squash, broth, apple, onion, brown sugar, sage and ginger in **CROCK-POT®** slow cooker.

2. Cover; cook on LOW 6 hours or on HIGH 3 hours or until squash is tender.

3. Purée soup in food processor or blender. Stir in cream just before serving.

Makes 6 to 8 servings

Tip: *For thicker soup, use only 3 cups chicken broth.*

Fiesta Black Bean Soup

6 **cups chicken broth**

12 **ounces potatoes, peeled and diced**

1 **can (15 ounces) black beans, rinsed and drained**

½ **pound cooked ham, diced**

½ **onion, diced**

1 **can (4 ounces) chopped jalapeño peppers**

2 **cloves garlic, minced**

2 **teaspoons dried oregano leaves**

1½ **teaspoons dried thyme leaves**

1 **teaspoon ground cumin**

Toppings: sour cream, chopped bell pepper and chopped tomatoes

1. Combine broth, potatoes, beans, ham, onion, jalapeño peppers, garlic, oregano, thyme and cumin in **CROCK-POT®** slow cooker; mix well.

2. Cover; cook on LOW 8 to 10 hours or on HIGH 4 to 5 hours.

3. Adjust seasonings. Serve with desired toppings.

Makes 6 to 8 servings

Double Corn Chowder

2 **small celery stalks, trimmed and chopped**

6 **ounces Canadian bacon, chopped**

1 **small onion** *or* **1 large shallot, chopped**

1 **serrano chile** *or* **jalapeño pepper, cored, seeded and minced***

1 **cup frozen corn, thawed**

1 **cup canned hominy**

¼ **teaspoon salt, or to taste**

¼ **teaspoon crushed dried thyme**

¼ **teaspoon black pepper, or to taste**

1 **cup chicken broth**

1 **tablespoon all-purpose flour**

1½ **cups milk, divided****

*Hot peppers can sting and irritate the skin, so wear rubber gloves when handling peppers and do not touch your eyes.

**For richer chowder, use ¾ cup milk and ¾ cup half-and-half.

1. Combine celery, Canadian bacon, onion, chile pepper, corn, hominy, salt, thyme and pepper in **CROCK-POT®** slow cooker. Add broth. Cover; cook on LOW 5 to 6 hours or on HIGH 3 to 3½ hours.

2. Turn **CROCK-POT®** slow cooker to LOW. Stir together flour and 2 tablespoons milk in small bowl. Stir into corn mixture. Add remaining milk. Cover; cook on LOW 20 minutes.

Makes 4 servings

Classic French Onion Soup

¼ **cup (½ stick) butter**

3 **large yellow onions, sliced**

1 **cup dry white wine**

3 **cans (about 14 ounces each) beef *or* chicken broth**

1 **teaspoon Worcestershire sauce**

½ **teaspoon salt**

½ **teaspoon dried thyme leaves**

4 **slices French bread, toasted**

1 **cup (4 ounces) shredded Swiss cheese**

Fresh thyme (optional)

1. Melt butter in large skillet over medium heat. Add onions, cook and stir 15 minutes or until onions are soft and lightly browned. Stir in wine.

2. Combine onion mixture, broth, Worcestershire sauce, salt and thyme in **CROCK-POT®** slow cooker. Cover; cook on LOW 4 to 4½ hours.

3. Ladle soup into 4 bowls; top each with bread slice and cheese. Garnish with fresh thyme, if desired.

Makes 4 servings

Celery-Leek Bisque

3 bunches leeks (about 3 pounds), trimmed*

2 medium stalks celery, sliced

1 medium carrot, peeled and sliced

3 cloves garlic, minced

2 cans (about 14 ounces each) fat-free chicken broth

1 package (8 ounces) cream cheese with garlic and herbs

2 cups half-and-half, plus more for garnish

Salt and black pepper

Fresh basil leaves (optional)

*It is very important to rinse leeks thoroughly before using. The gritty sand in which leeks are grown can become trapped between the layers of leaves and can be difficult to see. Cut trimmed leeks in half lengthwise and submerge in several inches of cool water several times to rinse off any trapped sand.

1. Combine leeks, celery, carrots, garlic and broth in **CROCK-POT®** slow cooker. Cover and cook on LOW 8 hours or on HIGH 4 hours.

2. Purée until smooth in blender, 1 cup at a time, returning batches to **CROCK-POT®** slow cooker as they are processed. Add cream cheese to last batch in blender and purée until smooth; stir cream cheese mixture and 2 cups half-and-half into soup. Add salt and pepper to taste. Serve immediately, or cool to room temperature and refrigerate in airtight container (flavors intensify overnight). Reheat before serving. Garnish with additional half-and-half and basil leaves, if desired.

Makes 4 to 6 servings

Pizza Soup

2 cans (14½ ounces each) stewed tomatoes with Italian seasonings, undrained

2 cups beef broth

1 cup sliced mushrooms

1 small onion, chopped

1 tablespoon tomato paste

¼ teaspoon salt, or to taste

¼ teaspoon black pepper, or to taste

½ pound turkey Italian sausage, casings removed

Shredded mozzarella cheese

1. Combine tomatoes with juice, broth, mushrooms, onion, tomato paste, salt and pepper in **CROCK-POT®** slow cooker.

2. Shape sausage into marble-size balls. Gently stir into soup mixture. Cover; cook on LOW 6 to 7 hours. Adjust salt and pepper, if necessary. Serve with cheese.

Makes 4 servings

Vegetable Medley Soup

3 cans (about 14 ounces each) chicken broth

3 sweet potatoes, peeled and chopped

3 zucchini, chopped

2 cups chopped broccoli

2 white potatoes, peeled and shredded

1 onion, chopped

1 stalk celery, finely chopped

1 teaspoon black pepper

¼ cup (½ stick) butter, melted

2 cups half-and-half *or* milk

1 tablespoon salt

1 teaspoon ground cumin

1. Combine chicken broth, sweet potatoes, zucchini, broccoli, white potatoes, onion, celery, butter and pepper in **CROCK-POT®** slow cooker.

2. Cover; cook on LOW 8 to 10 hours or on HIGH 4 to 5 hours.

3. Add half-and-half, salt and cumin. Cover; cook 30 minutes to 1 hour or until heated through.

Makes 12 servings

FLAVORS OF THE WORLD

Greek Lemon and Rice Soup

3 cans (about 14 ounces each) chicken broth

½ cup long-grain white rice (not converted or instant rice)

3 egg yolks

¼ cup fresh lemon juice

¼ teaspoon salt

⅛ teaspoon ground white pepper*

4 thin slices lemon (optional)

4 teaspoons finely chopped parsley (optional)

Substitute black pepper if desired.

1. Stir chicken broth and rice together in **CROCK-POT®** slow cooker. Cover and cook on HIGH 2 to 3 hours or until rice is cooked.

2. Turn to LOW. Whisk egg yolks and lemon juice together in medium bowl. Whisk large spoonful of hot rice mixture into egg yolk mixture. Whisk back into **CROCK-POT®** slow cooker.

3. Cook on LOW 10 minutes. Season with salt and pepper. Ladle soup into serving bowls and garnish each bowl with thin slice of lemon and 1 teaspoon chopped parsley, if desired.

Makes 4 servings

Note: *Soup may be served hot or cold. To serve cold, allow soup to cool to room temperature. Cover and refrigerate up to 24 hours before serving.*

French Lentil Rice Soup

6 cups chicken broth *or* vegetable broth

1 cup lentils, picked over and rinsed

2 medium carrots, peeled and finely diced

1 small onion, finely chopped

2 stalks celery, finely diced

3 tablespoons uncooked white rice

2 tablespoons minced garlic

1 teaspoon herbes de Provence *or* 1 teaspoon dried thyme

½ teaspoon salt

⅛ teaspoon ground white pepper*

¼ cup heavy cream *or* ¼ cup sour cream, divided (optional)

¼ cup chopped parsley (optional)

Substitute black pepper, if desired.

1. Stir together broth, lentils, carrots, onion, celery, rice, garlic, herbes de Provence, salt and pepper in **CROCK-POT®** slow cooker. Cover and cook on LOW 8 hours or on HIGH 4 to 5 hours.

2. Remove 1½ cups soup and purée in food processor or blender until almost smooth.* Stir puréed soup back into **CROCK-POT®** slow cooker.

3. Divide soup evenly among four serving bowls garnishing each with 1 tablespoon cream and 1 tablespoon chopped parsley, if desired.

Makes 4 servings

Use caution when processing hot liquids in blender. Vent lid of blender and cover with clean kitchen towel as directed by manufacturer.

Italian Hillside Garden Soup

1 tablespoon extra-virgin olive oil

1 cup chopped green bell pepper

1 cup chopped onion

½ cup sliced celery

1 can (about 14 ounces) diced tomatoes with basil, garlic and oregano, undrained

1 can (15½ ounces) navy beans, drained and rinsed

1 medium zucchini, chopped

1 cup frozen cut green beans, thawed

2 cans (about 14 ounces each) chicken broth

¼ teaspoon garlic powder

1 package (9 ounces) refrigerated sausage- *or* cheese-filled tortellini pasta

3 tablespoons chopped fresh basil

Grated Asiago or Parmesan cheese (optional)

1. Heat oil in large skillet over medium-high heat until hot. Add bell pepper, onion and celery. Cook and stir 4 minutes or until onions are translucent. Transfer to **CROCK-POT®** slow cooker.

2. Add tomatoes with juice, navy beans, zucchini, green beans, broth and garlic powder. Cover; cook on LOW 7 hours or on HIGH 3½ hours.

3. Turn **CROCK-POT®** slow cooker to HIGH. Add tortellini and cook 20 to 25 minutes longer or until pasta is tender. Stir in basil. Garnish each serving with cheese, if desired.

Makes 6 servings

Tip: *Cooking times are guidelines. CROCK-POT® slow cookers, just like ovens, cook differently depending on a variety of factors, including capacity. For example, cooking times will be longer at higher altitudes.*

Niku Jaga (Japanese Beef Stew)

2 tablespoons vegetable oil

2 pounds beef stew meat, cut in 1-inch cubes

4 medium carrots, peeled and sliced diagonally

3 medium Yukon Gold potatoes, peeled and chopped

1 white onion, peeled and chopped

1 cup water

½ cup Japanese sake *or* ½ cup dry white wine

¼ cup sugar

¼ cup soy sauce

1 teaspoon salt

1. Heat oil in skillet over medium heat until hot. Sear beef on all sides, turning as it browns. Transfer beef to **CROCK-POT®** slow cooker. Add remaining ingredients. Stir well to combine.

2. Cover; cook on LOW 10 to 12 hours or on HIGH 4 to 6 hours.

Makes 6 to 8 servings

Tuscany Bean and Prosciutto Soup

2 tablespoons unsalted butter

4 slices prosciutto*

3 cups water

1 cup dried navy beans, rinsed and sorted

½ cup dried lima beans, rinsed and sorted

1 medium yellow onion, finely chopped

1 tablespoon chopped fresh cilantro

1 teaspoon salt

1 teaspoon ground cumin

1 teaspoon black pepper

½ teaspoon ground paprika

2 cans (15 ounces each) diced tomatoes, undrained

*Substitute 4 slices bacon, if desired

1. Melt butter in large skillet over medium-high heat. Add prosciutto and fry until crisp. Remove to paper towels to cool.

2. Crumble prosciutto into small pieces in **CROCK-POT®** slow cooker. Add water, navy beans, lima beans, onion, cilantro, salt, cumin, black pepper and paprika. Stir well to combine. Cover and cook on LOW 10 to 12 hours.

3. Add tomatoes and juice and stir well. Cover and cook on HIGH 30 to 40 minutes or until soup is heated through.

Makes 6 servings

Russian Borscht

4 cups thinly sliced green cabbage

1½ pounds fresh beets, shredded

5 small carrots, halved lengthwise then cut into 1-inch pieces

1 parsnip, peeled, halved lengthwise then cut into 1-inch pieces

1 cup chopped onion

4 cloves garlic, minced

1 pound beef stew meat, cut into ½-inch cubes

1 can (about 14 ounces) diced tomatoes

3 cans (about 14 ounces each) reduced-sodium beef broth

¼ cup lemon juice, or more to taste

1 tablespoon sugar, or more to taste

1 teaspoon black pepper

Sour cream (optional)

Fresh parsley (optional)

1. Layer ingredients in **CROCK-POT®** slow cooker in following order: cabbage, beets, carrots, parsnip, onion, garlic, beef, tomatoes, broth, lemon juice, sugar and pepper. Cover; cook on LOW 7 to 9 hours or until vegetables are crisp-tender.

2. Season with additional lemon juice and sugar, if desired. Dollop each serving with sour cream and sprinkle with parsley, if desired.

Makes 12 servings

Fresh Lime and Black Bean Soup

2 cans (15 ounces each) black beans, undrained

1 can (14½ ounces) reduced-sodium chicken broth

1½ cups chopped onion

1½ teaspoons chili powder

¾ teaspoon ground cumin

¼ teaspoon garlic powder

⅛ to ¼ teaspoon red pepper flakes

½ cup sour cream

2 tablespoons extra-virgin olive oil

2 tablespoons chopped cilantro

1 medium lime, cut into wedges

1. Coat **CROCK-POT®** slow cooker with nonstick cooking spray. Add beans, broth, onion, chili powder, cumin, garlic powder and pepper flakes. Cover; cook on LOW 7 hours or on HIGH 3½ hours, or until onions are very soft.

2. Process 1 cup soup mixture in blender until smooth and return to **CROCK-POT®** slow cooker. Stir, check consistency, and repeat with additional 1 cup soup, as needed to achieve desired consistency. Let stand 15 to 20 minutes before serving.

3. Ladle soup into 4 bowls. Divide sour cream, oil and cilantro evenly among servings. Squeeze juice from lime wedge over each.

Makes 4 servings

Tip: *Brighten the flavor of dishes cooked in the CROCK-POT® slow cooker by adding fresh herbs or fresh lemon or lime juice just before serving.*

Minestrone alla Milanese

1 cup diced red potatoes

1 cup coarsely chopped carrots

1 cup coarsely chopped green cabbage

1 cup sliced zucchini

¾ cup chopped onion

¾ cup sliced fresh green beans

¾ cup coarsely chopped celery

¾ cup water

2 tablespoons olive oil

1 clove garlic, minced

½ teaspoon dried basil

¼ teaspoon dried rosemary

1 bay leaf

2 cans (about 14 ounces each) beef broth

1 can (about 14 ounces) diced tomatoes, undrained

1 can (15 ounces) cannellini beans, drained and rinsed

Shredded Parmesan cheese (optional)

1. Combine all ingredients except cannellini beans and cheese in **CROCK-POT®** slow cooker; mix well. Cover; cook on LOW 5 to 6 hours.

2. Add cannellini beans. Cover; cook on LOW 1 hour or until vegetables are tender.

3. Remove and discard bay leaf. Garnish with cheese, if desired.

Makes 8 to 10 servings

Irish Stew

1 cup fat-free reduced-sodium chicken broth

1 teaspoon dried marjoram

1 teaspoon dried parsley flakes

¾ teaspoon salt

½ teaspoon garlic powder

¼ teaspoon black pepper

1¼ pounds white potatoes, peeled and cut into 1-inch pieces

1 pound lean lamb for stew, cut into 1-inch cubes

8 ounces frozen cut green beans, thawed

2 small leeks, cut lengthwise into halves, then crosswise into slices

1½ cups coarsely chopped carrots

1. Combine broth, marjoram, parsley, salt, garlic powder and pepper in large bowl; mix well. Transfer to **CROCK-POT®** slow cooker.

2. Layer potatoes, lamb, green beans, leeks and carrots into **CROCK-POT®** slow cooker. Cover; cook on LOW 7 to 9 hours or until lamb is tender.

Makes 6 servings

Tip: *If desired, thicken cooking liquid with a mixture of 1 tablespoon cornstarch and ¼ cup water. Stir mixture into cooking liquid; cook on HIGH 10 to 15 minutes or until thickened.*

FLAVORS OF THE WORLD

Mediterranean Shrimp Soup

2 cans (14½ ounces each)
   fat-free reduced-sodium
   chicken broth

1 can (14½ ounces) diced
   tomatoes

1 can (8 ounces) tomato
   sauce

1 medium onion, chopped

½ medium green bell pepper,
   chopped

½ cup orange juice

½ cup dry white wine
   (optional)

1 jar (2½ ounces) sliced
   mushrooms

¼ cup sliced pitted black
   olives

2 cloves garlic, minced

1 teaspoon dried basil

2 bay leaves

¼ teaspoon whole fennel
   seeds, crushed

⅛ teaspoon black pepper

1 pound medium raw
   shrimp, peeled and
   deveined

1. Place all ingredients except shrimp in **CROCK-POT®** slow cooker. Cover; cook on LOW 4 to 4½ hours or until vegetables are crisp-tender.

2. Stir in shrimp. Cover; cook 15 to 30 minutes or until shrimp are pink and opaque. Remove and discard bay leaves.

Makes 6 servings

Note: *For a heartier soup, add 1 pound of firm white fish (such as cod or haddock), cut into 1-inch pieces, 45 minutes before end of cooking time.*

Pumpkin Soup with Crumbled Bacon and Toasted Pumpkin Seeds

2 teaspoons olive oil

½ cup raw pumpkin seeds*

3 slices thick-cut bacon

1 medium onion, chopped

1 teaspoon kosher salt

½ teaspoon chipotle chili powder, or more to taste

2 cans (29 ounces each) 100% pumpkin purée

4 cups chicken broth

¾ cup apple cider

½ cup whipping cream *or* half-and-half

Sour cream (optional)

*Raw pumpkin seeds may be found in the produce or ethnic food section of your local supermarket. They may be labeled "pepitas".

1. Spray inside of **CROCK-POT**® slow cooker with cooking spray.

2. In small skillet, heat olive oil over medium-high heat. Add pumpkin seeds to olive oil and stir until seeds begin to pop, about 1 minute. Spoon into small bowl and set aside.

3. Add bacon to skillet and cook until crisp. Remove bacon to paper towels and set aside to cool (do not drain drippings from pan). Reduce heat to medium and add onion to pan. Cook, stirring occasionally, until translucent, about 3 minutes. Stir in salt, chipotle chili powder and black pepper. Transfer to **CROCK-POT**® slow cooker.

4. Whisk pumpkin, chicken broth and apple cider into **CROCK-POT**® slow cooker, whisking until smooth.

5. Cover and cook on HIGH 4 hours. Turn off **CROCK-POT**® slow cooker and remove lid. Whisk in cream and adjust seasoning as necessary. Strain soup into bowls and garnish with pumpkin seeds, cooled bacon (crumbled) and sour cream, if desired.

Makes 4 servings

Black Bean Chipotle Soup

1 pound dry black beans

2 stalks celery, cut into ¼-inch dice

2 carrots, cut into ¼-inch dice

1 yellow onion, cut into ¼-inch dice

2 chipotle peppers in adobo sauce, chopped

1 cup crushed tomatoes

1 can (4 ounces) diced mild green chiles, drained

6 cups chicken *or* vegetable stock

2 teaspoons cumin

Salt and black pepper, to taste

Optional toppings: sour cream, chunky-style salsa, fresh chopped cilantro

1. Rinse and sort beans and place in large bowl; cover completely with water. Soak 6 to 8 hours or overnight. (To quick-soak beans, place beans in large saucepan; cover with water. Bring to a boil over high heat. Boil 2 minutes. Remove from heat; let soak, covered, 1 hour.) Drain beans; discard water.

2. Place beans in **CROCK-POT®** slow cooker. Add celery, carrots and onion.

3. Combine chipotles, tomatoes, chiles, stock and cumin in medium bowl. Add to **CROCK-POT®** slow cooker. Cover; cook on LOW 7 to 8 hours or on HIGH 4½ to 5 hours, or until beans are tender. Season with salt and pepper.

4. If desired, process mixture in blender, in 2 or 3 batches, to desired consistency, or leave chunky. Serve with sour cream, salsa and cilantro, if desired.

Makes 4 to 6 servings

Tip: *For an even heartier soup stir in 1 cup diced, browned spicy sausage, such as linguiça or chorizo, before serving.*

Pork and Anaheim Stew

2 tablespoons extra-virgin olive oil, divided

1½ pounds boneless pork shoulder, fat trimmed, cut into ½-inch pieces

6 Anaheim peppers, halved lengthwise, seeded and sliced*

4 cloves garlic, minced

1 pound tomatillos, papery skins removed, rinsed and chopped

2 cups chopped onion

1 can (15½ ounces) yellow hominy, rinsed and drained

1 can (about 14 ounces) fat-free chicken broth

2 teaspoons chili powder

1 teaspoon ground cumin

1 teaspoon dried oregano

1½ teaspoons sugar

1 teaspoon liquid smoke

½ teaspoon salt plus more to taste

*Anaheim peppers can sting and irritate the skin, so wear rubber gloves when handling peppers and do not touch your eyes.

1. Heat 1 teaspoon olive oil in large skillet over high heat. Add half pork and cook, stirring frequently, until browned on all sides. Transfer pork to **CROCK-POT®** slow cooker. Drain drippings from skillet and repeat with 1 teaspoon oil and remaining pork.

2. Reduce heat to medium-high. Add 1 teaspoon oil, turn ventilation fan to HIGH and add Anaheim peppers. Cook and stir 5 minutes or until peppers begin to brown on edges. Add garlic to peppers and cook 15 seconds, stirring constantly. Stir into pork in **CROCK-POT®** slow cooker. Stir in tomatillos, onion, hominy, chicken broth, chili powder, cumin, oregano, and sugar. Cover and cook on LOW 10 hours or on HIGH 5 hours.

3. Stir in remaining 1 tablespoon oil, liquid smoke and salt. Serve immediately or cover and refrigerate overnight (flavors intensify with time).

Makes 4 servings

DINNER IN A BOWL

Hearty Mushroom and Barley Soup

- 9 cups chicken broth
- 1 package (16 ounces) sliced fresh button mushrooms
- 1 large onion, chopped
- 2 carrots, chopped
- 2 stalks celery, chopped
- ½ cup uncooked pearl barley
- ½ ounce dried porcini mushrooms
- 3 cloves garlic, minced
- 1 teaspoon salt
- ½ teaspoon dried thyme
- ½ teaspoon black pepper

Combine all ingredients in **CROCK-POT®** slow cooker; stir until well blended. Cover; cook on LOW 4 to 6 hours.

Makes 8 to 10 servings

Variation: *For even more flavor, add a beef or ham bone to the CROCK-POT® slow cooker with the rest of the ingredients.*

Rich and Hearty Drumstick Soup

2 turkey drumsticks (about 1¾ pounds total)

2 medium carrots, peeled and sliced

1 medium stalk celery, thinly sliced

1 cup chopped onion

1 teaspoon minced garlic

½ teaspoon poultry seasoning

4½ cups chicken broth

2 ounces uncooked dry egg noodles

¼ cup chopped parsley

2 tablespoons butter

¾ teaspoon salt, or to taste

1. Coat **CROCK-POT®** slow cooker with nonstick cooking spray. Add drumsticks, carrots, celery, onion, garlic and poultry seasoning. Pour broth over; cover. Cook on HIGH 5 hours or until turkey meat is falling off bones.

2. Remove turkey; set aside. Add noodles to **CROCK-POT®** slow cooker; cover and cook 30 minutes more or until noodles are tender. Meanwhile, debone turkey and cut meat into bite-size pieces; set meat aside.

3. When noodles are cooked, stir in turkey, parsley, butter and salt.

Makes 4 servings

Hearty Meatball Stew

3 pounds ground beef *or* ground turkey

1 cup Italian bread crumbs

4 eggs

½ cup milk

¼ cup grated Romano cheese

2 teaspoons salt

2 teaspoons garlic salt

2 teaspoons black pepper

2 tablespoons olive oil

2 cups water

2 cups beef broth

1 can (14½ ounces) stewed tomatoes, undrained

1 can (12 ounces) tomato paste

1 cup chopped carrots

1 cup chopped onions

¼ cup chopped celery

1 tablespoon Italian seasoning

1. Combine beef, bread crumbs, eggs, milk, cheese, salt, garlic salt and pepper in large bowl. Form into 2-inch-round balls. Heat oil in skillet over medium-high heat until hot. Brown meatballs on all sides. Transfer to **CROCK-POT®** slow cooker.

2. Add remaining ingredients. Stir well to combine. Cover; cook on LOW 4 to 6 hours or on HIGH 2 to 4 hours.

Makes 6 to 8 servings

Northwoods Smoked Ham and Bean Soup

2 tablespoons olive oil

2 large onions, chopped

6 cloves garlic, peeled and minced

6 cups chicken stock

2 smoked ham hocks

2 cups cubed cooked smoked ham

1 can (28 ounces) whole peeled plum tomatoes, drained and coarsely chopped

1 bunch fresh parsley, stemmed and chopped

4 sprigs fresh thyme

4 bay leaves

2 cans (15 ounces each) cannellini beans, drained and rinsed

½ pound cooked orecchiette, cavatelli *or* ditalini pasta

Kosher salt and black pepper

1. Heat olive oil in skillet over medium heat. Add onions and cook, stirring occasionally, until soft and fragrant, about 10 minutes. Add garlic and cook 1 minute.

2. Place onion and garlic mixture, stock, ham hocks, ham, tomatoes, parsley, thyme and bay leaves in **CROCK-POT®** slow cooker. Cook on LOW 10 hours or on HIGH 6 hours.

3. Stir in beans and pasta and continue to cook on high until heated through.

4. Season to taste with salt and pepper and serve.

Makes 6 to 8 servings

Hearty Lentil and Root Vegetable Stew

2 cans (about 14 ounces each) chicken broth

1½ cups diced turnip

1 cup dried red lentils, rinsed and sorted

1 medium onion, cut into ½-inch wedges

2 medium carrots, cut into 1-inch pieces

1 medium red bell pepper, cut into 1-inch pieces

½ teaspoon dried oregano

⅛ teaspoon red pepper flakes

1 tablespoon olive oil

½ teaspoon salt

4 slices bacon, crisp-cooked and crumbled

½ cup finely chopped green onions

1. Combine broth, turnips, lentils, onion, carrots, bell pepper, oregano and pepper flakes in **CROCK-POT®** slow cooker. Cover; cook on LOW 6 hours or on HIGH 3 hours or until lentils are cooked.

2. Stir in olive oil and salt. Sprinkle each serving with bacon and green onions.

Makes 8 servings

DINNER IN A BOWL

Cape Cod Stew

½ **pound uncooked shrimp, peeled, cleaned and deveined**

½ **pound fresh cod** *or* **other white fish**

1 **pound mussels or hard-shell clams**

2 **cans (14½ ounces each) diced tomatoes, undrained**

4 **cups beef broth**

½ **cup chopped onions**

½ **cup chopped carrots**

½ **cup chopped cilantro**

2 **tablespoons sea salt**

2 **teaspoons crushed or minced garlic**

2 **teaspoons lemon juice**

4 **whole bay leaves**

1 **teaspoon dried thyme**

½ **teaspoon saffron**

1. Cut shrimp and fish into bite-size chunks and place in large bowl; refrigerate. Place mussels in second large bowl and set aside in refrigerator.

2. Combine remaining ingredients in **CROCK-POT®** slow cooker. Cover; cook on LOW 7 hours.

3. Add seafood. Cover; cook on HIGH 15 to 30 minutes or until seafood is just cooked through.

Makes 8 servings

Nana's Mini Meatball Soup

1 **pound ground beef**

1 **pound ground pork**

1½ **cups finely grated Pecorino Romano** *or* **Parmesan cheese**

1 **cup Italian bread crumbs**

2 **eggs**

1 **bunch flat-leaf parsley**

Kosher salt and black pepper

3 **quarts chicken stock**

1 **bunch escarole, coarsely chopped**

½ **box (8 ounces) ditalini pasta, cooked**

1. Combine beef, pork, cheese, bread crumbs, eggs, parsley, salt and pepper in large bowl. Mix well by hand and roll into ¾-inch meatballs.

2. Add meatballs and chicken stock to **CROCK-POT®** slow cooker. Cook on LOW 9 hours or on HIGH 5 hours.

3. Add escarole and cook until escarole has wilted and is bright green and tender, about 15 minutes. Add cooked ditalini to soup and serve.

Makes 6 to 8 servings

My Mother's Sausage and Vegetable Soup

1 can (15 ounces) black beans, drained and rinsed

1 can (about 14 ounces) diced tomatoes

1 can (10¾ ounces) condensed cream of mushroom soup, undiluted

½ pound smoked turkey sausage, cut into ½-inch slices

2 cups diced potato

1 cup chopped onion

1 cup chopped red bell pepper

½ cup water

2 teaspoons extra-hot prepared horseradish

2 teaspoons honey

1 teaspoon dried basil

Combine all ingredients in **CROCK-POT®** slow cooker, mix well. Cover; cook on LOW 7 to 8 hours or until potato is tender.

Makes 6 to 8 servings

DINNER IN A BOWL

Linguiça & Green Bean Soup

1 large yellow onion, chopped

3 cloves garlic, minced

2 tablespoons olive oil

1 cup tomato juice

4 cups water

1 tablespoon Italian seasoning

2 teaspoons garlic salt

1 teaspoon ground cumin

1 bay leaf

2 cans (16 ounces each) cut green beans, drained

1 can (16 ounces) kidney beans, drained

1 pound linguiça sausage, cooked and cut into bite-sized pieces

Place all ingredients in **CROCK-POT®** slow cooker. Cover; cook on LOW 8 to 10 hours or on HIGH 4 to 6 hours. Add more boiling water during cooking, if necessary.

Makes 6 servings

Tip: *Serve with warm cornbread.*

Navy Bean Bacon Chowder

1½ **cups dried navy beans**

2 **cups cold water**

6 **slices thick-cut bacon**

1 **medium carrot, cut lengthwise into halves, then cut into 1-inch pieces**

1 **small turnip, cut into 1-inch pieces**

1 **stalk celery, chopped**

1 **medium onion, chopped**

1 **teaspoon Italian seasoning**

⅛ **teaspoon black pepper**

1 **can (46 ounces) reduced-sodium chicken broth**

1 **cup milk**

1. Soak beans overnight in cold water; drain.

2. Cook bacon in medium skillet over medium heat. Drain fat; crumble bacon into **CROCK-POT®** slow cooker. Stir in beans, carrot, turnip, celery, onion, Italian seasoning and pepper. Add broth. Cover; cook on LOW 8 to 9 hours or until beans are tender.

3. Ladle 2 cups of soup mixture into food processor or blender. Process until smooth; return to **CROCK-POT®** slow cooker. Add milk. Cover; cook on HIGH 15 minutes or until heated through.

Makes 6 servings

Beggar's Chowder

¼ cup unsalted butter, at room temperature

¼ cup all-purpose flour

1 tablespoon garlic salt

1 tablespoon thyme

1 tablespoon sweet Hungarian paprika

½ teaspoon coarsely ground black pepper

4 skinless bone-in turkey legs or thighs, trimmed of visible fat

2 cans (14½ ounces each) cream-style sweet corn

1 can (10¾ ounces) condensed chicken broth, undiluted

1½ cups diced yellow onion

1 cup diced red bell pepper

1 cup diced green bell pepper

1 pound cleaned, stemmed white mushrooms, halved or quartered if large

1 can (14½ ounces) petite diced tomatoes, drained

1½ cups heavy whipping cream

½ cup chopped cilantro or parsley, plus additional for garnish

Salt and black pepper, to taste

1. Coat **CROCK-POT®** slow cooker with nonstick cooking spray. Combine butter, flour, garlic salt, thyme, paprika and pepper in small bowl. Use back of wooden spoon to work mixture into smooth paste. Rub paste into all sides of turkey.

2. Place turkey in **CROCK-POT®** slow cooker. Add corn, broth, onion and bell peppers.

3. Cover; cook on HIGH 3 hours or until turkey is fork-tender. Remove turkey; set aside until cool enough to handle.

4. Add mushrooms and tomatoes to cooking liquid. Cover; cook on HIGH 30 minutes longer.

5. Meanwhile, remove turkey meat from bones in bite-size pieces. When mushrooms are tender, return turkey to **CROCK-POT®** slow cooker. Add cream and cilantro. Cook, covered, about 15 minutes or until heated through. Add salt and pepper, if desired. Garnish with additional chopped cilantro, if desired.

Makes 8 servings

Mushroom Barley Stew

8 to 10 cups chicken *or* mushroom stock

1 cup pearl barley, rinsed and sorted (about ½ pound)

1 package (10 ounces) fresh mushrooms, such as cremini, rinsed and thinly sliced

1 cup dried mushrooms, porcini if possible, soaked to cover in warm water to soften, liquid reserved

2 carrots, peeled and cut into ¼-inch dice

2 celery stalks, cut into ¼-inch dice

1 yellow onion, cut into ¼-inch dice

1 tablespoon fresh thyme

2 bay leaves

1 tablespoon tomato paste

Salt and black pepper, to taste

2 tablespoons minced fresh parsley

1. Combine stock, barley, mushrooms, reserved mushroom liquid (taking care to discard any grit), carrots, celery, onion, thyme, bay, tomato paste, salt and black pepper in **CROCK-POT®** slow cooker.

2. Cover; cook on LOW 5½ hours or on HIGH 3 to 4 hours, or until barley and vegetables are tender. Add hot stock if needed during cooking.

3. Adjust seasonings. Garnish with parsley.

Makes 8 to 10 servings

Black Bean and Turkey Stew

3 cans (15 ounces each) black beans, rinsed and drained

1½ cups chopped onions

1½ cups fat-free reduced-sodium chicken broth

1 cup sliced celery

1 cup chopped red bell pepper

4 cloves garlic, minced

1½ teaspoons dried oregano leaves

¾ teaspoon ground coriander

½ teaspoon ground cumin

¼ teaspoon ground red pepper

6 ounces cooked turkey sausage, thinly sliced

1. Combine all ingredients except sausage in **CROCK-POT®** slow cooker. Cover; cook on LOW 6 to 8 hours.

2. Transfer about 1½ cups bean mixture from **CROCK-POT®** slow cooker to blender or food processor; purée bean mixture. Return to slow cooker. Stir in sausage. Cover; cook on LOW an additional 10 to 15 minutes.

Makes 6 servings

Hot Pot Noodle Soup

2 to 3 tablespoons peanut oil

2 large onions, chopped

1 large carrot, peeled and chopped

3 stalks lemongrass, thinly sliced

⅔ cup peeled and minced fresh ginger

8 garlic cloves, peeled and minced

7 whole star anise

3 quarts (12 cups) beef stock

3 tablespoons fish sauce (nam pla)*

1 package (12 ounces) fresh udon noodles *or* fresh linguini

1 tablespoon sesame oil

3 cups bean sprouts

4 green onions, thinly sliced

4 serrano chiles, thinly sliced

6 tablespoons chopped fresh basil

6 tablespoons chopped fresh mint

6 tablespoons chopped fresh cilantro

Lime wedges for serving

*Nam pla, Vietnamese fish sauce, can be found in the ethnic section of many grocery stores and in Asian markets.

1. Heat peanut oil in heavy large pot over medium-high heat. Add onions, carrot, lemongrass, ginger, garlic and star anise. Cook, stirring, until vegetables are softened. Transfer mixture to **CROCK-POT®** slow cooker. Add stock and fish sauce. Cover and cook on LOW 7 to 9 hours or on HIGH 4 to 5 hours. Remove star anise. Taste and adjust seasonings as desired.

2. Cook noodles in large pot of boiling salted water until tender. Drain; rinse under cold water. Return to same pot. Toss noodles with sesame oil.

3. To serve, place noodles in individual bowls, top with bean sprouts, green onions, chiles, basil, mint and cilantro. Ladle soup over noodles and serve with lime wedges.

Tip: *Try this with pork, chicken or seafood, infusing the appropriate stock with the aromatic herbs and spices.*

Makes 6 to 8 servings

85

HEARTY BEEF RECIPES

Hamburger Veggie Soup

1 pound 95% lean ground beef

1 bag (16 ounces) frozen mixed vegetables

1 package (10 ounces) frozen seasoning-blend vegetables*

1 can (10¾ ounces) condensed tomato soup, undiluted

1 can (about 14 ounces) stewed tomatoes, undrained

2 cans (5½ ounces each) spicy vegetable juice

Salt and black pepper

*Seasoning-blend vegetables are a mixture of chopped bell peppers, onions and celery. If you're unable to find frozen vegetables, use ½ cup of each fresh vegetable.

Coat **CROCK-POT®** slow cooker with nonstick cooking spray. Crumble beef before placing in bottom. Add remaining ingredients. Stir well to blend. Cover; cook on HIGH 4 hours. If necessary, break up large pieces of beef. Add salt and pepper before serving, if desired.

Makes 4 to 6 servings

Asian Beef Stew

2 onions, cut into ¼-inch slices

1½ pounds round steak, sliced thin across the grain

2 stalks celery, sliced

2 carrots, peeled and sliced *or* 1 cup peeled baby carrots

1 cup sliced mushrooms

1 cup orange juice

1 cup beef broth

⅓ cup hoisin sauce*

2 tablespoons cornstarch

1 to 2 teaspoons Chinese five-spice powder* *or* curry powder

1 cup frozen peas

Hot cooked rice

Chopped fresh cilantro (optional)

Available in the Asian foods aisle of your local market.

1. Place onions, beef, celery, carrots and mushrooms in **CROCK-POT®** slow cooker.

2. Combine orange juice, broth, hoisin sauce, cornstarch and five-spice powder in small bowl. Pour into **CROCK-POT®** slow cooker. Cover; cook on HIGH 5 hours or until beef is tender.

3. Stir in peas. Cook 20 minutes longer or until peas are tender. Serve with hot cooked rice, and garnish with cilantro, if desired.

Makes 6 servings

HEARTY BEEF RECIPES

Grandma Ruth's Minestrone

1 pound ground beef

1 cup dried red kidney
   beans

1 package (16 ounces)
   frozen mixed vegetables

2 cans (8 ounces each)
   tomato sauce

1 can (about 14 ounces)
   diced tomatoes, undrained

¼ head shredded cabbage

1 cup chopped onions

1 cup chopped celery

½ cup chopped fresh parsley

1 tablespoon dried basil

1 tablespoon Italian
   seasoning

1 teaspoon salt

1 teaspoon black pepper

1 cup cooked macaroni

1. Combine ground beef and beans in **CROCK-POT®** slow cooker. Cover; cook on HIGH 2 hours.

2. Add all remaining ingredients except macaroni and stir to blend. Cover; cook on LOW for 6 to 8 hours or until beans are tender.

3. Stir macaroni into slow cooker. Cover; cook on HIGH for 1 hour.

Makes 4 servings

Beef Stew

½ cup all-purpose flour

1 teaspoon salt

1 teaspoon black pepper

4 pounds beef chuck, cut into 1-inch cubes

Olive oil

1 ½ cups red *or* white wine

1 cup beef broth

2 onions, sliced

1 cup sliced mushrooms

1 cup flat-leaf parsley, minced

6 teaspoons minced garlic

4 whole bay leaves

1. Mix flour, salt and pepper. Dredge beef in flour. Heat oil in skillet over medium heat until hot. Sear beef on all sides, turning as it browns. Transfer to **CROCK-POT®** slow cooker.

2. Add remaining ingredients and stir well to combine. Cover; cook on LOW 4 to 6 hours or on HIGH 2 to 3 hours.

Makes 6 to 8 servings

HEARTY BEEF RECIPES

Sweet and Sour Brisket Stew

1 jar (12 ounces) chili sauce

1½ to 2 tablespoons packed dark brown sugar

1½ tablespoons fresh lemon juice

¼ cup beef broth

1 tablespoon Dijon mustard

¼ teaspoon paprika

½ teaspoon salt, or to taste

¼ teaspoon black pepper, or to taste

1 clove garlic, minced

1 small onion, chopped

1 well-trimmed beef brisket, cut into 1-inch pieces*

2 large carrots, cut into ½-inch slices

1 tablespoon all-purpose flour (optional)

Beef brisket has a heavy layer of fat, which some supermarkets trim off. If the meat is trimmed, buy 2½ pounds; if not, purchase 4 pounds, then trim and discard excess fat.

1. Combine sauce, 1½ tablespoons brown sugar, lemon juice, broth, mustard, paprika, salt and pepper in **CROCK-POT®** slow cooker. (Add remaining sugar, if desired, after tasting.)

2. Add garlic, onion, beef and carrots. Stir well to coat. Cover; cook on LOW 8 hours.

3. If thicker gravy is desired, whisk together 1 tablespoon flour and 3 tablespoons cooking liquid in small bowl. Add to **CROCK-POT®** slow cooker. Cover; cook on HIGH 10 minutes, or until thickened.

Makes 6 to 8 servings

HEARTY BEEF RECIPES

Beef Fajita Soup

1 **pound beef stew meat**

1 **can (15 ounces) pinto beans, drained and rinsed**

1 **can (15 ounces) black beans, drained and rinsed**

1 **can (about 14 ounces) diced tomatoes with roasted garlic, undrained**

1 **can (about 14 ounces) beef broth**

1 **small green bell pepper, thinly sliced**

1 **small red bell pepper, thinly sliced**

1 **small onion, thinly sliced**

1½ **cups water**

2 **teaspoons ground cumin**

1 **teaspoon seasoned salt**

1 **teaspoon black pepper**

1. Combine beef, beans, tomatoes with juice, broth, bell peppers, onion, water, cumin, salt and black pepper in **CROCK-POT®** slow cooker.

2. Cover; cook on LOW 8 hours.

Makes 8 servings

Serving Suggestion: *Serve topped with sour cream, shredded Monterey Jack or Cheddar cheese and chopped olives.*

HEARTY BEEF RECIPES

Mexican Cheese Soup

1 **pound processed cheese, cubed**

1 **pound ground beef, cooked and drained**

1 **can (8¾ ounces) whole kernel corn, undrained**

1 **can (15 ounces) kidney beans, undrained**

1 **jalapeño pepper, seeded and diced* (optional)**

1 **can (14½ ounces) diced tomatoes with green chiles, undrained**

1 **can (14½ ounces) stewed tomatoes, undrained**

1 **envelope taco seasoning**

* Jalapeño peppers can sting and irritate the skin; wear rubber gloves when handling peppers and do not touch eyes. Wash hands after handling.

1. Coat inside of **CROCK-POT®** slow cooker with nonstick cooking spray. Combine cheese, beef, corn, beans with liquid, jalapeño, if desired, tomatoes with chiles, stewed tomatoes and taco seasoning in prepared **CROCK-POT®** slow cooker.

2. Cover; cook on LOW 4 to 5 hours or on HIGH 3 hours or until done.

Makes 6 to 8 servings

Serving Suggestion: *Corn chips make an excellent accompaniment to this hearty soup.*

Wild Mushroom Beef Stew

1½ **to 2 pounds beef stew meat, cut into 1-inch cubes**

2 **tablespoons all-purpose flour**

½ **teaspoon salt**

½ **teaspoon black pepper**

1½ **cups beef broth**

1 **teaspoon Worcestershire sauce**

1 **clove garlic, minced**

1 **bay leaf**

1 **teaspoon paprika**

4 **shiitake mushrooms, sliced**

2 **medium carrots, sliced**

2 **medium potatoes, diced**

1 **small white onion, chopped**

1 **stalk celery, sliced**

1. Place beef in **CROCK-POT®** slow cooker. Mix together flour, salt and pepper and sprinkle over beef; stir to coat evenly. Add remaining ingredients and stir to mix well.

2. Cover; cook on LOW 10 to 12 hours or on HIGH for 4 to 6 hours. Stir the stew before serving.

Makes 5 servings

Note: *This classic beef stew is given a twist with the addition of flavorful shiitake mushrooms. If shiitake mushrooms are unavailable in your local grocery store, you can substitute other mushrooms of your choice. For extra punch, add a few dried porcini mushrooms to the stew.*

Tip: *You may double the amount of meat, mushrooms, carrots, potatoes, onion and celery for a 5-, 6- or 7-quart* **CROCK-POT®** *slow cooker.*

Chuck and Stout Soup

2 tablespoons olive oil

3 pounds beef chuck, cut into 1-inch cubes

Kosher salt and black pepper

8 cups beef stock

3 large onions, thinly sliced

3 stalks celery, diced

6 carrots, peeled and diced

4 cloves garlic, peeled and minced

2 packages (10 ounces each) cremini mushrooms, thinly sliced

1 package (about 1 ounce) dried porcini mushrooms, processed to a fine powder

4 sprigs fresh thyme

1 bottle (12 ounces) stout beer

Flat-leaf parsley to garnish

1. Heat oil in skillet over medium-high to high heat. Season meat with salt and pepper. In two batches, brown beef on all sides, taking care to not crowd meat. Meanwhile, in large saucepan, bring beef stock to a boil and reduce by half.

2. Remove beef and place in **CROCK-POT®** slow cooker. Add reduced stock and all remaining ingredients except parsley. Cover and cook on LOW 10 hours or on HIGH 6 hours.

3. Garnish with parsley and serve.

Makes 6 to 8 servings

Note: *A coffee grinder works best for processing dried mushrooms, but a food processor or blender can also be used.*

Hamburger Soup

1 **pound lean ground beef**

1 **cup thinly sliced carrots**

1 **cup sliced celery**

1 **package (1 ounce) dry onion soup mix**

1 **package (1 ounce) Italian salad dressing mix**

¼ **teaspoon seasoned salt**

¼ **teaspoon black pepper**

3 **cups boiling water**

1 **can (about 14 ounces) diced tomatoes, undrained**

1 **can (8 ounces) tomato sauce**

1 **tablespoon soy sauce**

2 **cups cooked macaroni**

¼ **cup grated Parmesan cheese**

2 **tablespoons chopped fresh parsley**

1. Brown ground beef in large skillet 6 to 8 minutes over medium-high heat, stirring to break up meat. Drain fat.

2. Place carrots and celery in **CROCK-POT®** slow cooker. Top with beef, soup mix, salad dressing mix, seasoned salt and pepper. Add water, tomatoes with juice, tomato sauce and soy sauce; mix well. Cover; cook on LOW 6 to 8 hours.

3. Stir in macaroni and Parmesan cheese. Cover; cook on HIGH 15 to 30 minutes or until heated through. Sprinkle with parsley just before serving.

Makes 6 to 8 servings

Beef Stew with Bacon, Onion and Sweet Potatoes

1 **pound beef for stew, cut into 1-inch chunks**

1 **can (14½ ounces) beef broth**

2 **medium sweet potatoes, peeled and cut into 2-inch chunks**

1 **large onion, cut into 1½-inch chunks**

2 **slices thick-cut bacon, diced**

1 **teaspoon dried thyme**

1 **teaspoon salt**

¼ **teaspoon black pepper**

2 **tablespoons cornstarch**

2 **tablespoons water**

1. Coat **CROCK-POT®** slow cooker with nonstick cooking spray. Combine all ingredients, except cornstarch and water, in **CROCK-POT®** slow cooker; mix well. Cover; cook on LOW 7 to 8 hours or on HIGH 4 to 5 hours, or until meat and vegetables are tender.

2. With slotted spoon, transfer beef and vegetables to serving bowl; cover with foil to keep warm.

3. Turn **CROCK-POT®** slow cooker to HIGH. Combine cornstarch and water; stir until smooth. Stir into cooking liquid. Cover; cook 15 minutes or until thickened. To serve, spoon sauce over beef and vegetables.

Makes 4 servings

French Beef Bourguignon

2 tablespoons vegetable oil

2 pounds boneless beef chuck roast, cut into 1-inch pieces

4 medium carrots, cut into thin, 4-inch pieces

1 can (14½ ounces) diced tomatoes, undrained

1 small yellow onion, diced

2 stalks celery, sliced

1 cup chopped white button mushrooms

1 cup dry red wine

1 tablespoon chopped fresh thyme leaves

1 teaspoon salt

1 teaspoon minced fresh basil

1 teaspoon dry mustard

¼ teaspoon ground black pepper

2 tablespoons flour

¼ cup water

1 pound homestyle noodles, cooked according to package directions (optional)

1. Heat oil in large skillet over medium-high heat. Add half the beef and cook, turning to brown all sides. Transfer to **CROCK-POT®** slow cooker and repeat with remaining beef.

2. Add carrots, tomatoes and juice, onion, celery, mushrooms, red wine, thyme, salt, basil, dry mustard and black pepper. Stir to combine. Cover and cook on LOW 8 to 10 hours or on HIGH 4 to 5 hours, or until vegetables and beef are very tender and sauce is rich.

3. Thirty minutes before serving whisk flour into water in small bowl until smooth and combined. Stir into sauce. Turn to HIGH and cook until flour and water thicken sauce, about 3 to 5 minutes. Serve over hot cooked noodles, if desired.

Makes 8 servings

Beef Stew with Molasses and Raisins

⅓ cup all-purpose flour

2 teaspoons salt, divided

1½ teaspoons black pepper, divided

2 pounds beef stew meat, cut into 1½-inch pieces

5 tablespoons oil, divided

2 medium onions, sliced

1 can (28 ounces) diced tomatoes, drained

1 cup beef broth

3 tablespoons molasses

2 tablespoons cider vinegar

4 cloves garlic, minced

2 teaspoons dried thyme

1 teaspoon celery salt

1 bay leaf

8 ounces baby carrots, cut in half lengthwise

2 parsnips, diced

½ cup golden raisins

1. Combine flour, 1½ teaspoons salt and 1 teaspoon pepper in large bowl. Toss meat in flour mixture. Heat 2 tablespoons oil in large skillet or Dutch oven over medium-high heat until hot. Add half of beef and brown on all sides. Set aside browned beef and repeat with 2 additional tablespoons oil and remaining beef.

2. Add remaining 1 tablespoon oil to skillet. Add onions and cook, stirring to loosen any browned bits, about 5 minutes. Add tomatoes, broth, molasses, vinegar, garlic, thyme, celery salt, bay leaf and remaining ½ teaspoon salt and ½ teaspoon pepper. Bring to a boil. Add browned beef and boil 1 minute.

3. Transfer to **CROCK-POT®** slow cooker. Cover; cook on LOW 5 hours or on HIGH 2½ hours. Add carrots, parsnips and raisins. Cook 1 to 2 hours longer or until vegetables are tender. Remove and discard bay leaf.

Makes 6 to 8 servings

CHICKEN SOUPS

Country Chicken Chowder

2 tablespoons margarine
or butter

1½ pounds boneless, skinless chicken breast tenders, cut into ½-inch pieces

2 small onions, chopped

2 stalks celery, sliced

2 small carrots, peeled and sliced

2 cups frozen corn

2 cans (10¾ ounces each) condensed cream of potato soup, undiluted

1½ cups chicken broth

1 teaspoon dried dill weed

½ cup half-and-half

1. Melt margarine in large skillet. Add chicken; cook until browned.

2. Add cooked chicken, onions, celery, carrots, corn, soup, chicken broth and dill to **CROCK-POT®** slow cooker. Cover and cook on LOW 3 to 4 hours or until chicken is no longer pink and vegetables are tender.

3. Turn off heat; stir in half-and-half. Cover and let stand 5 to 10 minutes or just until heated through.

Makes 8 servings

Note: *For a special touch, garnish soup with croutons and fresh dill.*

CHICKEN SOUPS

Chicken Soup

6 cups chicken broth

1½ pounds boneless skinless chicken breasts, cubed

2 cups sliced carrots

1 cup sliced mushrooms

1 red bell pepper, chopped

1 onion, chopped

2 tablespoons grated fresh ginger

3 teaspoons minced garlic

½ teaspoon crushed red pepper

Salt and black pepper, to taste

Place all ingredients in **CROCK-POT®** slow cooker. Cover; cook on LOW 6 to 7 hours or on HIGH 3 to 3½ hours.

Makes 4 to 6 servings

CHICKEN SOUPS

Creamy Farmhouse Chicken and Garden Soup

½ (16-ounce) package frozen pepper stir-fry vegetable mix

1 cup frozen corn

1 medium zucchini, sliced

2 bone-in chicken thighs, skinned

½ teaspoon minced garlic

1 can (about 14 ounces) fat-free chicken broth

½ teaspoon dried thyme

2 ounces uncooked egg noodles

1 cup half-and-half

½ cup frozen green peas, thawed

2 tablespoons chopped parsley

2 tablespoons butter, melted

1 teaspoon salt

½ teaspoon coarsely ground black pepper

1. Coat **CROCK-POT®** slow cooker with nonstick cooking spray. Place stir-fry vegetables, corn and zucchini in bottom. Add chicken, garlic, broth and thyme. Cover; cook on HIGH 3 to 4 hours or until chicken is no longer pink. Remove chicken and set aside to cool slightly.

2. Add noodles to **CROCK-POT®** slow cooker. Cover; cook 20 minutes longer, or until noodles are done.

3. Meanwhile, debone and chop chicken. Return to **CROCK-POT®** slow cooker. Stir in remaining ingredients. Let stand 5 minutes before serving.

Makes 4 servings

Note: *To skin chicken easily, grasp skin with paper towel and pull away. Repeat with fresh paper towel for each piece of chicken, discarding skins and towels.*

Chicken Miso Soup with Shiitake Mushrooms

16 chicken thighs (about 5 pounds) with skin and bone

3 to 4 cups chicken stock

3 tablespoons canola oil

2 large onions, coarsely chopped

1 pound fresh shiitake mushrooms, stems discarded, large caps quartered

3 tablespoons finely chopped peeled ginger

3 tablespoons finely chopped garlic

1 cup mirin (Japanese sweet rice wine)

1 cup white miso paste

½ cup soy sauce

4 cups water

1 pound (about 16 cups) mustard greens, tough stems and ribs discarded and leaves coarsely chopped

Cooked white rice (optional)

Thinly sliced green onions, for garnish

1. Preheat oven to 500°F with rack in middle.

2. Pat chicken dry, then roast, skin side up, in 1 layer on 17 × 12-inch rimmed sheet pan or jelly-roll pan with sides until skin is golden brown, 35 to 40 minutes.

3. Transfer roasted chicken and pan liquids to bowl and spoon off fat that rises to surface. Add enough stock to bring liquid to 4 cups total.

4. Heat oil in skillet over medium heat and sauté onions until softened and beginning to brown. Add mushrooms, ginger and garlic, and sauté until garlic is golden, 3 to 5 minutes.

5. Add mirin to pan and bring to a boil, stirring and scraping up any brown bits for 1 minute. Pour into **CROCK-POT®** slow cooker. Stir in miso paste and soy sauce, then add chicken, stock mixture and water. Cover and cook on LOW 8 to 9 hours or on HIGH 4 to 5 hours or until chicken is tender.

6. Stir in mustard greens and continue to cook, covered, 5 minutes or until greens are wilted. Taste and adjust seasonings as desired. Serve in shallow bowls with cooked white rice, if desired, and garnish with green onions.

Makes 6 to 8 servings

Hearty Chicken Tequila Soup

1 small onion, cut into
  8 wedges

1 cup frozen corn, thawed

1 can (14½ ounces) diced
  tomatoes with mild green
  chiles, undrained

2 cloves garlic, minced

2 tablespoons chopped
  fresh cilantro, plus
  additional for garnish

1 whole chicken (about
  3½ pounds)

2 cups chicken broth

3 tablespoons tequila

¼ cup sour cream

1. Spread onions in bottom of **CROCK-POT®** slow cooker. Add corn, tomatoes with chiles, garlic and 2 tablespoons cilantro. Mix well to combine. Place chicken on top of tomato mixture.

2. Combine broth and tequila in medium bowl. Pour over chicken. Cover; cook on LOW 8 to 10 hours.

3. Transfer chicken to cutting board and let rest until cool enough to handle. Remove skin and bones. Pull meat apart with 2 forks into bite-size pieces. Return chicken to **CROCK-POT®** slow cooker and stir.

4. Serve with dollop of sour cream and garnish with cilantro.

Makes 2 to 4 servings

CHICKEN SOUPS

Hearty Chicken Noodle Soup

1¼ pounds boneless, skinless chicken breasts

1¼ pounds boneless, skinless chicken thighs

12 baby carrots, cut into ½-inch pieces

4 stalks celery, cut into ½-inch pieces

¾ cup finely chopped onion

1 teaspoon dried parsley flakes

½ teaspoon black pepper

¼ teaspoon cayenne pepper

1 teaspoon salt

4 cans (14½ ounces each) chicken broth

4 chicken-flavored bouillon cubes

2 cups uncooked egg noodles

1. Cut chicken into bite-size pieces. Place in **CROCK-POT®** slow cooker. Add carrots, celery, onion, parsley, black pepper, cayenne pepper, salt, chicken broth and bouillon cubes. Cover; cook on LOW 5 to 6 hours.

2. Stir in egg noodles. Turn temperature to HIGH. Cook 30 minutes longer or until noodles are tender.

Makes 8 to 10 servings

CHICKEN SOUPS

Chicken and Wild Rice Soup

3 cans (about 14 ounces each) chicken broth

1 pound boneless, skinless chicken breasts *or* thighs, cut into bite-size pieces

2 cups water

1 cup sliced celery

1 cup diced carrots

1 package (6 ounces) converted long grain and wild rice mix with seasoning packet (not quick-cooking or instant rice)

½ cup chopped onion

½ teaspoon black pepper

2 teaspoons white vinegar (optional)

1 tablespoon dried parsley flakes

1. Combine broth, chicken, water, celery, carrots, rice mix and seasoning packet, onion and pepper in **CROCK-POT®** slow cooker; mix well.

2. Cover; cook on LOW 6 to 7 hours or on HIGH 4 to 5 hours or until chicken is tender.

3. Stir in vinegar, if desired. Sprinkle with parsley.

Makes 9 servings

CHICKEN SOUPS

Vietnamese Chicken Pho

8 cups chicken stock

2 to 3 cups cooked chicken, shredded

8 ounces bean sprouts

Rice stick noodles

1 bunch Thai basil, chopped

Hoisin sauce, for serving

Lime wedges, for serving

1. Add stock and chicken to **CROCK-POT®** slow cooker. Cover and cook on LOW 6 to 7 hours or on HIGH 3 hours.

2. Add bean sprouts, noodles and Thai basil. Heat until noodles are softened.

3. Spoon soup into individual serving bowls and serve with hoisin sauce and lime wedges.

Makes 4 to 6 servings

Note: *A simple soup to prepare with leftover shredded chicken, this classic Asian chicken noodle soup packs tons of flavor.*

CHICKEN SOUPS

Chicken & Barley Soup

1 cup thinly sliced celery

1 medium onion, coarsely chopped

1 carrot, cut into thin slices

½ cup medium pearl barley

1 clove garlic, minced

1 cut-up whole chicken (about 3 pounds)

1 tablespoon olive oil

2½ cups chicken broth

1 can (about 14 ounces) diced tomatoes, undrained

¾ teaspoon salt

½ teaspoon dried basil

¼ teaspoon black pepper

1. Place celery, onion, carrot, barley and garlic in **CROCK-POT®** slow cooker.

2. Remove and discard skin from chicken pieces. Separate drumsticks from thighs. Trim back bone from breasts. Save wings for another use. Heat oil in large skillet over medium-high heat; brown chicken pieces on all sides. Place chicken in **CROCK-POT®** slow cooker.

3. Add broth, tomatoes with juice, salt, basil and pepper. Cook on LOW 7 to 8 hours or HIGH 4 hours or until chicken and barley are tender. Remove chicken and debone. Cut chicken into bite-size pieces; stir into soup.

Makes 4 servings

CHICKEN SOUPS

Tortilla Soup

2 cans (about 14 ounces each) chicken broth

1 can (about 14 ounces) diced tomatoes with jalapeño peppers

2 cups chopped carrots

2 cups frozen corn, thawed

1½ cups chopped onions

1 can (8 ounces) tomato sauce

1 tablespoon chili powder

1 teaspoon ground cumin

¼ teaspoon garlic powder

2 cups chopped cooked chicken (optional)

Shredded Monterey Jack cheese

Tortilla chips, broken

1. Combine broth, tomatoes, carrots, corn, onions, tomato sauce, chili powder, cumin and garlic powder in **CROCK-POT®** slow cooker. Cover; cook on LOW 6 to 8 hours.

2. Stir in chicken, if desired. Ladle into bowls. Top each serving with cheese and tortilla chips.

Makes 6 servings

Curried Chicken and Coconut Soup

6 cups chicken stock

2 cans (13½ ounces each) unsweetened coconut milk

2 bunches green onions, sliced

3 to 4 tablespoons curry powder

4 stalks lemongrass, minced

2 tablespoons peeled and minced fresh ginger

8 large chicken thighs with bones, skin removed

2 packages (6 ounces each) baby spinach leaves

3 large limes, divided

Salt and black pepper, to taste

1 bunch fresh cilantro, chopped

1. Combine stock, coconut milk, green onions, curry powder, lemongrass, ginger and chicken in **CROCK-POT®** slow cooker. Cook on LOW 10 hours or on HIGH 6 hours.

2. Remove chicken from **CROCK-POT®** slow cooker to cutting board; let rest for a few minutes.

3. Remove bones and cut chicken into ½-inch cubes. Return chicken to soup; add spinach. Cook on HIGH until spinach wilts, about 10 minutes. Juice 2 limes and add juice to **CROCK-POT®** slow cooker. Season soup to taste with salt and pepper. Cut remaining lime into 6 to 8 wedges. Ladle soup into individual serving bowls; sprinkle with cilantro and serve with lime wedges.

Makes 6 to 8 servings

Chicken Fiesta Soup

4 boneless, skinless chicken breasts, cooked and shredded

1 can (14½ ounces) stewed tomatoes, drained

2 cans (4 ounces each) chopped green chiles, drained

1 can (28 ounces) enchilada sauce

1 can (14½ ounces) chicken broth

1 cup finely chopped onions

2 cloves garlic, minced

1 teaspoon ground cumin

1 teaspoon chili powder

¾ teaspoon black pepper

1 teaspoon salt

¼ cup finely chopped fresh cilantro

1 cup frozen whole kernel corn

1 yellow squash, diced

1 zucchini, diced

8 tostada shells, crumbled

2 cups (8 ounces) shredded Cheddar cheese

1. Combine chicken, tomatoes, chiles, enchilada sauce, broth, onions, garlic, cumin, chili powder, pepper, salt, cilantro, corn, squash and zucchini, in **CROCK-POT®** slow cooker.

2. Cover; cook on LOW 8 hours. To serve, fill individual bowls with soup. Garnish with crumbled tostada shells and cheese.

Makes 8 servings

Matzo Ball Soup

3 quarts (12 cups) chicken stock

4 parsnips, peeled and sliced into ½-inch rounds

2 carrots, peeled and sliced into ½-inch rounds

3 leeks, sliced

1 large onion, sliced

1 small rotisserie chicken, cooked (optional)

1 tablespoon fresh dill

Matzo Balls (recipe follows)

Kosher salt and black pepper

1. Add stock to **CROCK-POT®** slow cooker. Add parsnips, carrots, leeks and onion to stock and cook on LOW 8 to 10 hours or on HIGH 4 to 5 hours.

2. Remove skin and bones from chicken and cut into bite-sized pieces. Add chicken, if desired, dill and Matzo Balls to hot soup and cook on HIGH until heated through. Season to taste with salt and pepper and serve.

Makes 4 to 6 servings

Matzo Balls

4 large eggs

5 tablespoons butter *or* margarine, melted

1 small bunch flat-leaf parsley, minced

1 tablespoon fresh sage, minced

1¼ cups matzo meal

½ cup water

Kosher salt and black pepper

1. Combine all ingredients in mixing bowl and blend with fork, making sure to generously season mixture with salt and pepper. Roll into golf ball-size or smaller matzo balls.

2. Cover and place in refrigerator 30 to 60 minutes.

3. Bring a pot of salted water to boil over medium-high heat. Drop matzo balls in and simmer for 20 minutes. Remove with a slotted spoon and reserve until needed.

INDEX

INDEX

INDEX

INDEX

INDEX

INDEX

METRIC CHART

VOLUME MEASUREMENTS (dry)

⅛ teaspoon = 0.5 mL
¼ teaspoon = 1 mL
½ teaspoon = 2 mL
¾ teaspoon = 4 mL
1 teaspoon = 5 mL
1 tablespoon = 15 mL
2 tablespoons = 30 mL
¼ cup = 60 mL
⅓ cup = 75 mL
½ cup = 125 mL
⅔ cup = 150 mL
¾ cup = 175 mL
1 cup = 250 mL
2 cups = 1 pint = 500 mL
3 cups = 750 mL
4 cups = 1 quart = 1 L

VOLUME MEASUREMENTS (fluid)

1 fluid ounce (2 tablespoons) = 30 mL
4 fluid ounces (½ cup) = 125 mL
8 fluid ounces (1 cup) = 250 mL
12 fluid ounces (1½ cups) = 375 mL
16 fluid ounces (2 cups) = 500 mL

WEIGHTS (mass)

½ ounce = 15 g
1 ounce = 30 g
3 ounces = 90 g
4 ounces = 120 g
8 ounces = 225 g
10 ounces = 285 g
12 ounces = 360 g
16 ounces = 1 pound = 450 g

DIMENSIONS

1/16 inch = 2 mm
⅛ inch = 3 mm
¼ inch = 6 mm
½ inch = 1.5 cm
¾ inch = 2 cm
1 inch = 2.5 cm

OVEN TEMPERATURES

250°F = 120°C
275°F = 140°C
300°F = 150°C
325°F = 160°C
350°F = 180°C
375°F = 190°C
400°F = 200°C
425°F = 220°C
450°F = 230°C

BAKING PAN AND DISH EQUIVALENTS

Utensil	Size in Inches	Size in Centimeters	Volume	Metric Volume
Baking or Cake Pan (square or rectangular)	8×8×2	20×20×5	8 cups	2 L
	9×9×2	23×23×5	10 cups	2.5 L
	13×9×2	33×23×5	12 cups	3 L
Loaf Pan	8½×4½×2½	21×11×6	6 cups	1.5 L
	9×9×3	23×13×7	8 cups	2 L
Round Layer Cake Pan	8×1½	20×4	4 cups	1 L
	9×1½	23×4	5 cups	1.25 L
Pie Plate	8×1½	20×4	4 cups	1 L
	9×1½	23×4	5 cups	1.25 L
Baking Dish or Casserole			1 quart/4 cups	1 L
			1½ quart/6 cups	1.5 L
			2 quart/8 cups	2 L
			3 quart/12 cups	3 L